Superstructures

TREMENDOUS
TUNNELS

Ian Graham

amicus
mankato, minnesota

Published by Amicus
P.O. Box 1329, Mankato, Minnesota 56002

Printed in the United States of America at Corporate
Graphics, in North Mankato, Minnesota.

Published by arrangement with the Watts Publishing Group
Ltd., London.

Library of Congress Cataloging-in-Publication Data
Graham, Ian, 1953-
   Tremendous tunnels / by Ian Graham.
      p. cm. -- (Superstructures)
   Includes index.
   Summary: "Describes some of the longest and most famous
   tunnels ever built. Includes information on the tunnel
   designers, the challenges they faced, and statistics of the
   finished tunnels"--Provided by publisher.
   ISBN 978-1-60753-134-0 (library binding)
   1. Tunnels--Juvenile literature. 2. Tunneling--Juvenile
literature. I. Title.
   TA807.G73 2011
   624.1'93--dc22
                                    2009030865

Editor: Michael Downey
Art Direction: Harleen Mehta (Q2AMedia)
Designer: Tarang Saggar (Q2AMedia)
Picture Researcher: Kamal Kumar (Q2AMedia)
Illustrators: Sibi ND and Danish Zaidi (Q2AMedia)

Picture credits:
t=top b=bottom c=center l=left r=right

Cover: SJ. Krasemann/ Photolibrary: Front, Aneese/
Dreamstime: Back

Title Page: Eurotunnel

Stephen Alvarez/ National Geographic/ Getty Images: 4,
Thomas Talbot Bury/ The Bridgeman Art Library/
Getty Images: 5tl, Corbis: 5cr, Ian Klein/ Shutterstock: 6, Rfx/
Shutterstock: 7, Bettmann/ Corbis: 8,
Mary Altaffer/ Associated Press: 9tl, Atlantide Phototravel/
Corbis: 9br, Robert Harding/ Photolibrary: 10, Stringer/
Getty Images: 11b, Bettmann/ Corbis: 12, Eurotunnel: 14,
Qaphotos.com/ Alamy: 15b, Jacques Langevin/ Corbis Sygma:
16, Massachusetts Turnpike Authority: 18–19, Nasa: 20, BLS
AlpTransit AG, Switzerland: 22–23, WIRTH: 24–25, SMART:
26–27.

Q2AMedia Art Bank: 5br, 11t, 13, 15t, 17, 21, 29.

Note to parents and teachers:
Every effort has been made by the publishers to ensure that
the web sites in this book are suitable for children,
that they are of the highest educational value, and that they
contain no inappropriate or offensive material.
However, because of the nature of the Internet, it is
impossible to guarantee that the contents of these sites will
not be altered. We strongly advise that Internet access is
supervised by a responsible adult.

1210
32010

9 8 7 6 5 4 3 2 1

CONTENTS

EARLY TUNNELS

A tunnel is a passageway through the ground. People have been building tunnels for thousands of years. The ancient Babylonians built a tunnel under the Euphrates River more than 4,000 years ago. It linked the royal palace with a temple on the other side of the river. The Romans built more tunnels than anyone else in the ancient world. Most were built to carry water into cities. The longest Roman tunnel was nearly 3.7 miles (6 km) long.

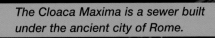
The Cloaca Maxima is a sewer built under the ancient city of Rome.

When completed, the Thames Tunnel in London was hailed as the "eighth wonder of the world."

Thames Tunnel

The first tunnel to be dug under a major river since ancient times was the Thames Tunnel, under the Thames River in London. Digging through the soft ground under the river was dangerous because the tunnel could collapse at any moment. The tunnel's designer, Marc Isambard Brunel, invented a **tunneling shield** to stop this from happening. It supported the tunnel while the workers dug out the earth. The shield then was pushed forward and the workers dug out more earth. The Thames Tunnel opened to the public in 1843.

Road Tunnels

When cars became more popular in the 1920s, tunnels were built to shorten journeys by taking roads under rivers and through hills. The 1.6 mile (2.6 km) Holland Tunnel was built at this time to carry traffic under the Hudson River in New York. It consists of two tubes, each with two **lanes** of traffic. During construction, the tunnel was sealed at both ends and air was pumped inside at a high pressure to keep river water out. The tunnel is still in use today.

The Holland Tunnel in New York opened in 1927 after seven years of construction work.

SHAPE OF A TUNNEL

Tunnels have to withstand the huge weight of rock and earth above them. The pressing action of the surrounding rock is called pressure. A tunnel has to be strong enough to keep its shape and to avoid being squashed! The deepest tunnels are usually circular, because a circular tunnel spreads the pressure evenly around the outside of the whole tunnel.

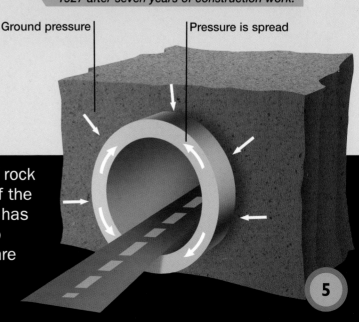

Ground pressure

Pressure is spread

NEW YORK CITY SUBWAY

With more than 8 million people, New York City is the largest city in the United States. Its vast **subway** is one of the world's largest underground railway systems and carries millions of people every day.

FACT FILE
- Length: 229 mi. (368 km)
- Where in the world: New York City
- When built: 1904
- Type: Subway
- Constructed by: Blasting, boring, and mining

New York City Subway trains travel through tunnels up to 197 feet (60 m) below street level.

A Growing City

The building of the subway system enabled the city of New York to expand. It provided people with a faster way of getting around by avoiding the slow and overcrowded roads, river **ferries**, and surface trains. In 1900, most of the city's 3.4 million people lived in Manhattan, one of the city's five boroughs. Very few people lived in the borough of Brooklyn. By 1914, thanks to the new subway, the population of Brooklyn had increased by almost 1 million.

Power to the System

The trains in the New York City Subway are powered by electricity that runs in a **third rail**. Power stations supply the subway with up to 27,000 volts. More than 200 electricity substations take this high-voltage supply and reduce it to 625 volts for the trains. The power is carried through the tunnels to more than 620 miles (1,000 km) of tracks by up to 2,485 miles (4,000 km) of electric cables.

AMAZING FACTS

Up to 6.4 million people ride the New York Subway on an average weekday. This amounts to more than a billion people each year.

The total length of the tracks, including the service lines, is 842 miles (1,355 km).

The New York City Subway uses enough electrical power to light up a city of 700,000 people.

About 40 percent of the subway system is above ground.

The subway trains run every four minutes during the rush hours.

Tunnels link the underground platforms.

Cut and Cover

The first part of the subway was built using the **cut-and-cover** method. The tunnels were built under streets wherever possible. The street was scraped off and the tunnel was dug below ground. Then the street was rebuilt over the top. Extra-strong supports were used when the tunnel passed under a big building. In wet ground, sheets of felt soaked in a sticky, oily liquid called asphalt were put behind the tunnel walls to help keep water out.

Diggers dug out the first subway tunnels, and then the street was put back on top.

AMAZING FACTS

When the New York City Subway opened on October 27, 1904, 150,000 people stood in line to pay five cents to ride one of the first subway trains.

The subway's deepest station is 191st Street. This is 197 feet (60 m) below street level.

A subway tunnel had to be built through the foundations of the New York Times building as the building went down deeper than the subway!

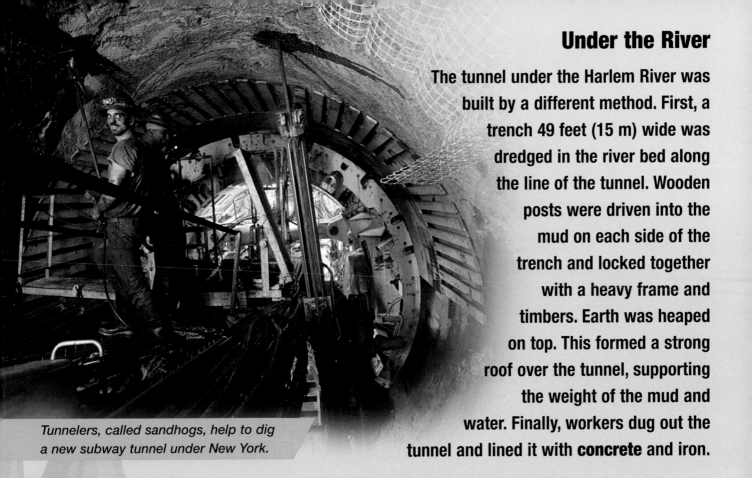

Under the River

The tunnel under the Harlem River was built by a different method. First, a trench 49 feet (15 m) wide was dredged in the river bed along the line of the tunnel. Wooden posts were driven into the mud on each side of the trench and locked together with a heavy frame and timbers. Earth was heaped on top. This formed a strong roof over the tunnel, supporting the weight of the mud and water. Finally, workers dug out the tunnel and lined it with **concrete** and iron.

Tunnelers, called sandhogs, help to dig a new subway tunnel under New York.

Mechanical Moles

Today, the first major expansion of the subway system for 50 years is under way. It is called the Second Avenue Project because it is being built under the city's Second Avenue. The project is due to be completed around the year 2020. Most of the new tunnels will be built without tearing up the streets. Giant machines will bore a massive hole the size of the tunnel through the ground without disturbing the street or buildings.

At street level, passageways provide travelers with access to 277 underground stations.

WATER TABLE

The natural level of water in the ground is known as the water table. As subways and other tunnels are often built below the water table, water drains continuously into the tunnels from the surrounding ground. It has to be removed or the tunnels would fill up with water. More than 700 pumps remove 13 million gallons (50 million L) of water from the subway on a dry day. When it rains, even more is pumped out.

MONT BLANC TUNNEL

The Mont Blanc Tunnel is an important road route through the Alps, one of the great mountain ranges of Europe. Connecting Chamonix in France with Courmayeur in Italy, it runs underneath Mont Blanc, the highest mountain in the Alps.

Rules for Traffic

The horseshoe-shaped Mont Blanc Tunnel has a 23 foot (7 m) wide, two-lane **roadway** with a 31 inch (80 cm) wide **walkway** on each side. Drivers must keep to a speed of 31–44 miles (50–70 km) per hour and keep at least 492 feet (150 m) between vehicles. Every 984 feet (300 m), drivers can pull in and stop at **lay-bys**.

FACT FILE
- Length: 7.2 mi. (11.6 km)
- Where in the world: Italy and France
- When built: 1965
- Type: Road
- Constructed by: Blasting and boring

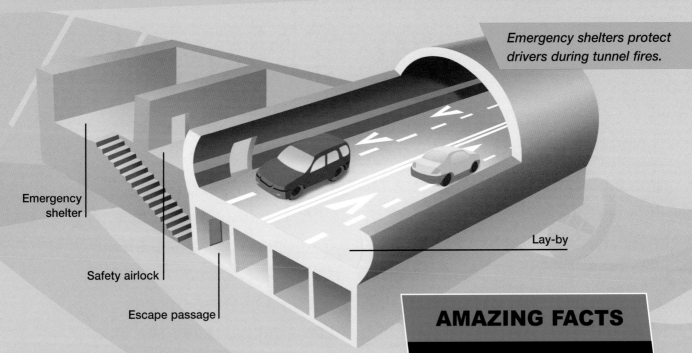

Emergency
shelter

Lay-by

Safety airlock

Escape passage

Video Surveillance

After a serious fire in the tunnel in 1999, in which
39 people died, safety standards were improved.
The tunnel was closed for three years while it was
repaired and upgraded. Sensors at each end of the
tunnel can now spot overheating vehicles that may
cause a fire before they enter the tunnel. Traffic
inside the tunnel is monitored by 120 video cameras.
A firefighting team is stationed in the tunnel 24 hours
a day. If a fire does break out, 116 smoke extractors
draw smoke out and keep the air clear.

*Mont Blanc Tunnel fire trucks
have a driver's cab on each end.*

AMAZING FACTS

The Mont Blanc Tunnel was
built by five engineers and
a workforce of 350 men. It
took eight years to complete.

More than 772 tons (700 t)
of explosives were used to
blast rock out of the tunnel.

Teams of tunnelers started
from the French and Italian
sides of the tunnel. When
the teams met in the middle,
the two tunnels were only
5 inches (13 cm) off target.

SEIKAN TUNNEL

The Seikan Tunnel is the world's longest railway tunnel. It runs under the Tsugaru Strait, a channel of water between the Japanese islands of Honshu and Hokkaido. The tunnel was built because strong winds and rough seas often made it impossible for passenger ferries to cross the **strait**. Bad weather closes the strait to ferries about 80 days every year. Although Japanese railway engineers first started thinking of building a tunnel under the strait in the 1930s, construction work did not begin until 1971.

Construction workers board a train to travel into the Seikan Tunnel.

FACT FILE

- Length: 33.4 mi. (53.8 km)
- Where in the world: Japan
- When built: 1988
- Type: Railway
- Constructed by: Blasting

Blasting and Filling

The rock underneath the Tsugaru Strait is probably the worst type for digging tunnels. It is crumbly and full of cracks that make it very weak in places and let water flow through. To construct the Seikan Tunnel, rock was blasted out with explosives. Then holes were drilled in the tunnel walls and a cement material called **grout** was pumped into the holes. The grout filled the cracks in the rock and made the walls stronger. Concrete was spread all over the walls before concrete **lining** blocks were fitted.

Three-in-one

The Seikan Tunnel is actually three tunnels. A small tunnel called a **pilot tunnel** was first dug to check how good, or bad, the rock was. After the main tunnel was completed, the pilot tunnel was used as a drain to collect water leaking into the main tunnel. A small **service tunnel** was dug alongside the main tunnel to carry workers and to provide an escape route for passengers in case of an emergency.

AMAZING FACTS

The deepest part of the tunnel is 328 feet (100 m) below the seabed, which is 787 feet (240 m) below the surface of the sea. The Seikan Tunnel is the world's deepest railway tunnel.

Pumps, which run 24 hours a day, keep the tunnel dry.

If the water pumps were to fail, the tunnel would fill up with water in three days.

Almost half of the Seikan Tunnel lies under the sea.

Volcanic rock

Service tunnel

Pilot tunnel

Twin-track railway line

Main railway tunnel

Connecting gallery

Honshu entrance

CHANNEL TUNNEL

The Channel Tunnel is a railway link between Britain and France that runs underneath the English Channel, the narrow sea channel between the two countries. When completed in 1994, the Channel Tunnel set several world records. These included the world's longest tunnel between two countries, the second-longest tunnel under water after the Seikan Tunnel, and the tunnel with the longest undersea section.

FACT FILE

- Length: 31.3 mi. (50.4 km)
- Where in the world: English Channel
- When built: 1994
- Type: Railway
- Constructed by: Boring

AMAZING FACTS

Every day, 500 sensors take 2.5 million measurements of the temperature, the water flow, and gas levels to ensure that conditions inside the Channel Tunnel are safe.

The rail tunnels are 24.9 feet (7.6 m) wide. The service tunnel is 15.7 feet (4.8 m) wide.

The 31 mile (50 km) journey takes 35 minutes. About 24 miles (38 km) of the tunnel is under the sea.

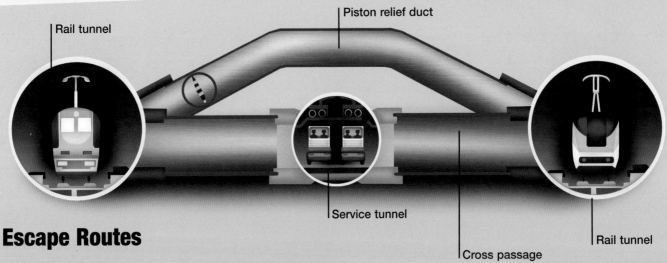

Rail tunnel

Piston relief duct

Service tunnel

Cross passage

Rail tunnel

Escape Routes

The Channel Tunnel is made up of three tunnels. Two main tunnels carry trains. A smaller service tunnel carries maintenance workers and provides an emergency escape route for travelers. Cross passages link the two rail tunnels with the service tunnel every 1,230 feet (375 m). Smaller cross-tunnels, called piston relief ducts, let the air pushed along in front of each train escape into the other tunnel.

The Channel Tunnel's rail and service tunnels are interconnected.

Smoke from a steam engine was used to test the Channel Tunnel's fire safety system.

Giant Caverns

The Channel Tunnel is protected by fire safety systems. If a fire is detected, the tunnel is closed while the fire is dealt with. Two huge underground caverns let trains cross from one tunnel to the other, so that only one section of a tunnel need be closed. The caverns are so big that four school buses could be stacked on top of each other inside a cavern. When the crossover caverns are not in use, giant sliding doors are closed between the tunnels.

A tunnel boring machine is lowered down a shaft to start tunneling through the ground.

Ideal for Tunneling

One of the layers of rock under the channel is called **chalk marl**. It is a mixture of chalk and clay and is ideal for tunneling. It is soft enough to dig through, but also strong enough to avoid collapsing. The tunnels were dug by 11 massive **tunnel boring machines**, which are known as TBMs. Each of the three tunnels were dug by two TBMs, each setting out from the opposite shores and meeting in the middle. The other TBMs dug the parts of the tunnels that lie under land.

AMAZING FACTS

The biggest TBMs were nearly 29.5 feet (9 m) across and weighed more than 1,650 tons (1,500 t). With the service train, they were 853 feet (260 m) long.

Giant fans pump 188 cubic yards (144 cu m) of fresh air into the tunnel every second.

Up to 311 miles (500 km) of cold water pipes absorb and carry away heat generated by the fast-moving trains.

Concrete Walls

The TBMs did not just dig, they also built the tunnel lining. This is the thick concrete wall that stops the tunnel from slowly collapsing under the weight of the ground and sea above. Powerful lifting gear raised heavy concrete blocks into place against the tunnel wall. Cement grout was then pumped behind the lining to fill any gaps.

Refreshing the Air

The air inside a long tunnel has to be refreshed continuously by fans so that it is fresh enough for people to breathe. In the Channel Tunnel, huge fans blow enough fresh air into the service tunnel for 20,000 people. The air then flows to the rail tunnels so that any smoke from a fire is blown away from the service tunnel where passengers would go to escape.

Rail tunnel

Cooling water pipes

Overhead power line

High-voltage cable

Main lighting

When construction work was complete, there was still a lot of work to be done installing power, lighting, and other services.

Service tunnel

Drainage pipes

Firefighting water pipe

Walkway

Railway track

Drain

Track support blocks

Service tunnel vehicle

Drain

Conveyor belt carries rock away

TUNNEL BORING MACHINES

A tunnel boring machine is a giant mechanical device that burrows through the ground. A revolving disc at the front is covered with metal teeth. As the disc turns, the teeth cut into the rock, which falls inside the machine. A conveyor belt moves it to the back and railway wagons carry it out of the tunnel.

Control cabin

Cutting head rotates

Robotic lining assembler

TED WILLIAMS TUNNEL

The Ted Williams Tunnel is one of three tunnels that form part of a huge building project in Boston, Massachusetts. The project is known as the **Big Dig**. It is the most complex engineering project in the history of the United States. It moved Boston's busiest highways underground.

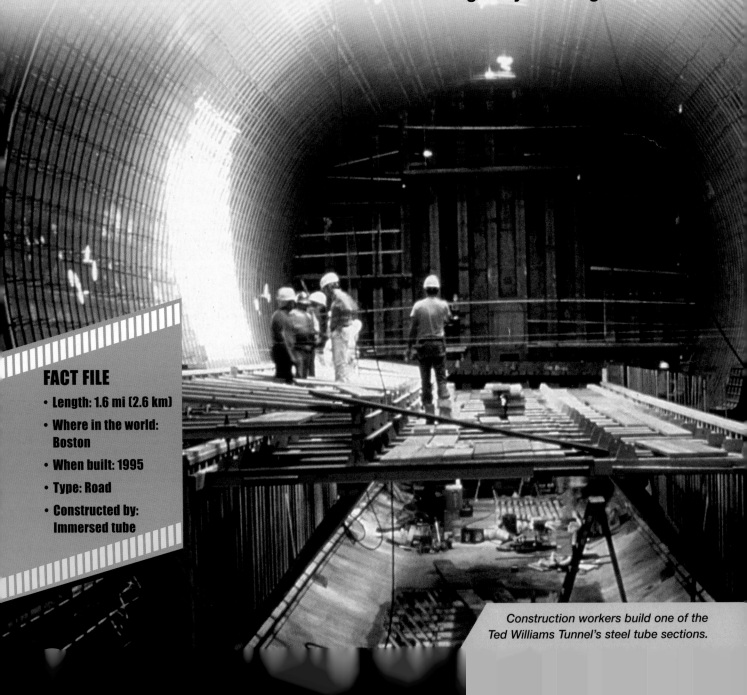

FACT FILE

- Length: 1.6 mi (2.6 km)
- Where in the world: Boston
- When built: 1995
- Type: Road
- Constructed by: Immersed tube

Construction workers build one of the Ted Williams Tunnel's steel tube sections.

The Ted Williams Tunnel, named after a famous Boston baseball player, routes traffic under Boston Harbor.

Tubes of Traffic

The Ted Williams Tunnel was made in steel sections. Each section has two tubes side by side. Each tube is big enough for two lanes of traffic. The sections were built in a shipyard and transported to Boston on **barges**. Then the concrete roads were installed. Finally, the twin-tube sections were lowered into a trench in the harbor floor and earth was piled on top of them.

Dealing with Spoil

One of the main problems faced by many tunnelers is what to do with all the earth and rock that is dug out to make the tunnel. This is called **spoil**. In the case of the Ted Williams Tunnel, the spoil dug out to create tunnels leading down to the tubes on the seabed was dumped on Spectacle Island. It covered an old rubbish dump, and a new public park was created.

ORESUND TUNNEL

The Oresund Tunnel is the world's largest **immersed tube** tunnel. It enables motorists to drive between Sweden and Denmark. The link between the two countries consists of three sections: a bridge, a manmade island, and a tunnel. The tunnel carries four lanes of road traffic and two railway tracks beneath the Drogden Channel.

FACT FILE
- Length: 2.3 mi. (3.7 km)
- Where in the world: Denmark
- When built: 2000
- Type: Road and railway
- Constructed by: Immersed tube

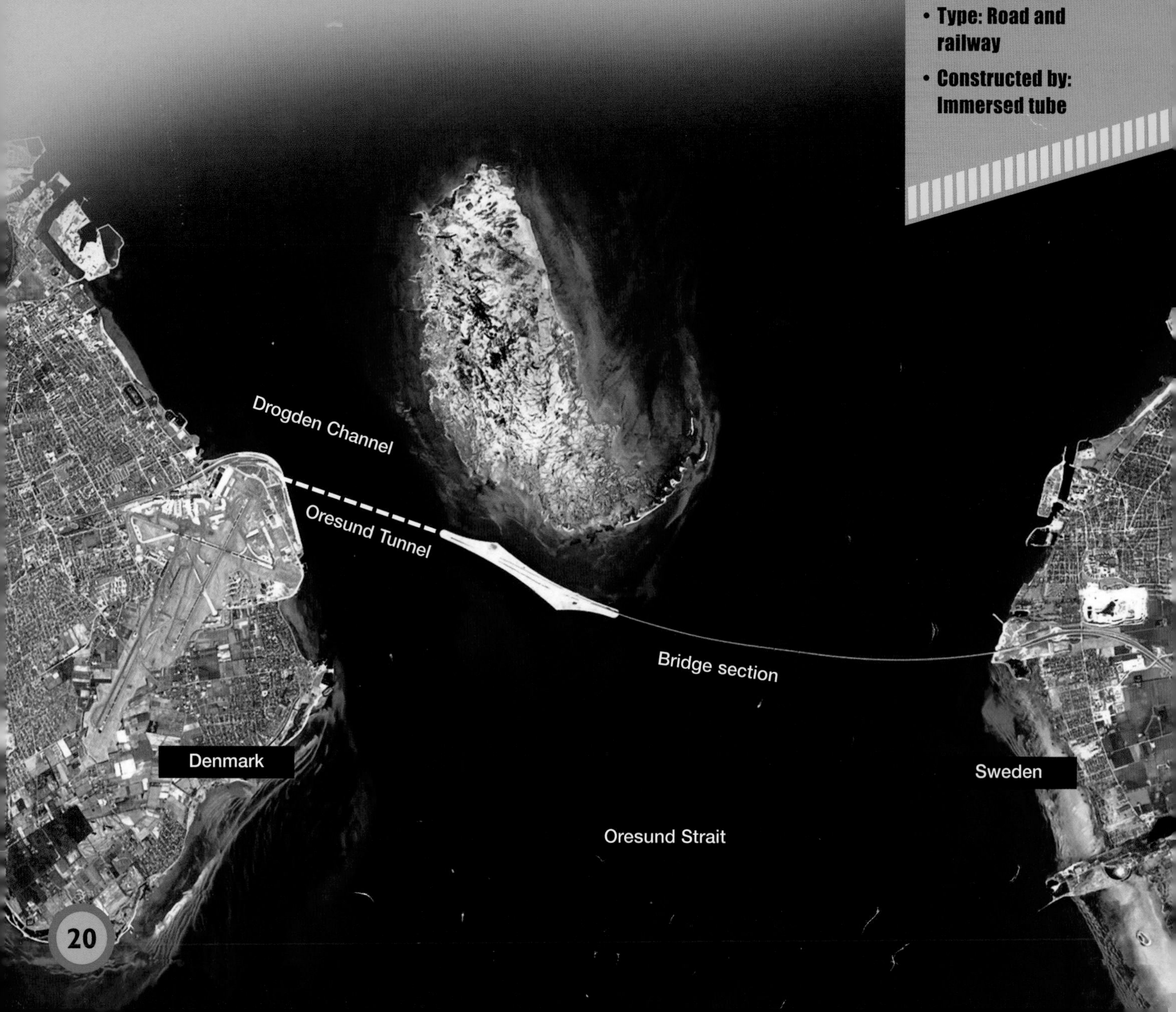

Drogden Channel

Oresund Tunnel

Bridge section

Denmark

Sweden

Oresund Strait

20

Making the Link

In 1991, the governments of Sweden and Denmark agreed to build a **fixed link** between their two countries. Tunnel boring machines could not be used to make the tunnel part of the link because the rock under the seabed was unsuitable. Instead, engineers decided to use the immersed tube method. In the tunnel, a four-lane road and two railway tracks are housed in four separate square tubes, which lie side by side on the seabed.

Sinking the Tunnel

The tunnel was cast in concrete sections on dry land. Each section contained two road tunnels and two rail tunnels. The sections, sealed at the ends to keep water out, were floated out to the right position and then unsealed and flooded with water to sink them into a trench in the seabed. The sections were joined together by divers, and the water was pumped out. Then the signs, lighting, safety systems, **ventilation**, and communications were installed.

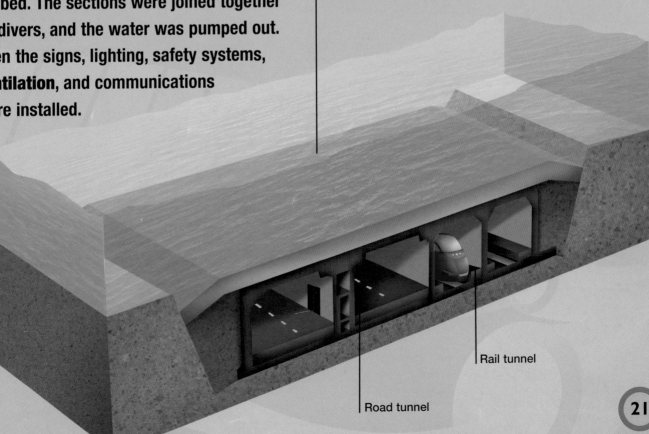

The Oresund Tunnel is the world's largest immersed tube tunnel.

Drogden Channel

Rail tunnel

Road tunnel

LÖTSCHBERG BASE TUNNEL

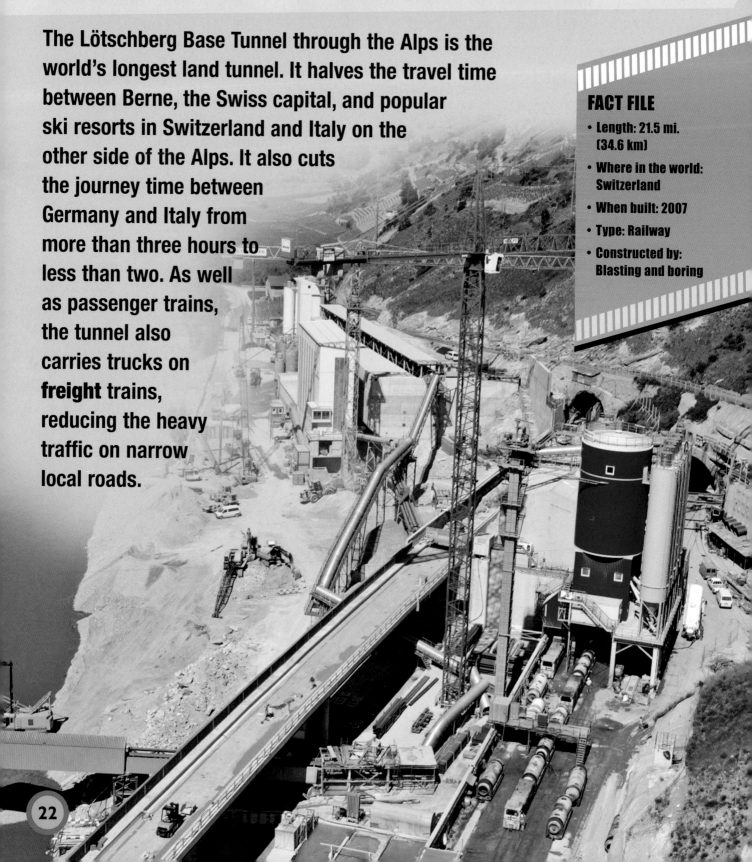

The Lötschberg Base Tunnel through the Alps is the world's longest land tunnel. It halves the travel time between Berne, the Swiss capital, and popular ski resorts in Switzerland and Italy on the other side of the Alps. It also cuts the journey time between Germany and Italy from more than three hours to less than two. As well as passenger trains, the tunnel also carries trucks on **freight** trains, reducing the heavy traffic on narrow local roads.

FACT FILE

- Length: 21.5 mi. (34.6 km)
- Where in the world: Switzerland
- When built: 2007
- Type: Railway
- Constructed by: Blasting and boring

Part of the tunnel was lined with wire mesh and covered with concrete.

Taking Turns

Tests on the ground through which the tunnel was to go showed that it was made of different types of rock including sandstone, slate, limestone and granite. The tunnel was divided into 11 sections, and each section was dug using the best method. About one-fifth of the tunnel was dug by tunnel boring machines. The rest was blasted with explosives. The original design was for two tunnels, side by side. So far, only one of the tunnels has been completed. Trains take turns to go through it in opposite directions.

Liquid Explosive

Deep holes for explosive charges were drilled by a machine called a **drilling jumbo**. This machine, which has several arms with drills on each end, drilled holes up to 14.8 feet (4.5 m) deep in the rock. Tunnel workers then filled the holes with liquid explosive, which they **detonated**. Each huge blast lengthened the tunnel by about 13 feet (4 m).

BORING OR BLASTING?

The choice of construction method depends on the type of rock a tunnel goes through, as well as the tunnel's length. A tunnel boring machine, or TBM, cuts a perfectly circular tunnel through the ground. TBMs are considered to be the best choice for long tunnels that lie in firm rock that is the same all the way. If the ground is not suitable for a tunnel boring machine, explosives are used.

Lötschberg Base Tunnel

GUADARRAMA TUNNEL

The Guadarrama Tunnel forms part of the Madrid–Segovia–Valladolid high-speed rail route in Spain. It is the fourth-longest railway tunnel in Europe and the fifth-longest in the world. The railway line through the tunnel is used by Spain's Alta Velocidad Española (AVE) high-speed trains. Going through the mountains, instead of over or around them, cuts the journey time across the Guadarrama Mountains from three hours to only 55 minutes.

FACT FILE
- Length: 17.6 mi. (28.4 km)
- Where in the world: Spain
- When built: 2007
- Type: Railway
- Constructed by: Boring

Staying on Course

The tunnel was built by four tunnel boring machines that dug two tubes, each 31.2 feet (9.5 m) across and 98 feet (30 m) apart. The TBMs tunneling toward each other from either end of the tunnel were steered through the hard granite rock. When they met in the middle, they were off target by less than 4 inches (10 cm). Not bad after tunneling 9 miles (15 km)!

A service train makes its way through the Guadarrama Tunnel during construction.

Safety Cross-tunnels

Long, twin-tube tunnels like this are connected by cross-tunnels. These cross-tunnels let people switch from one tunnel to the other on foot in an emergency. The Guadarrama twin tunnels are connected every 820 feet (250 m). During the tunnel's construction, cross-tunnels were dug every .6 mile (1 km) for the workers' safety. The remaining cross-tunnels were added later.

AMAZING FACTS

The Guadarrama Tunnel passes under Peñalara Peak, the highest mountain in the Guadarrama mountain range.

The maximum height of rock above the tunnel is 3,255 feet (992 m).

The tunnel entrance at the Madrid end is 3,274 feet (998 m) above sea level. The tunnel rises to 3,937 feet (1,200 m) above sea level.

With the lining installed, each of the twin tubes is 27.9 feet (8.5 m) wide.

Modern tunnel boring machines are fitted with a shield to support the tunnel.

Tunneling shield   Cutting head

TUNNELING SHIELD

A tunneling shield is a structure that protects workers, especially when they are tunneling through soft ground or broken rock that may collapse. The tunneling shield was invented in 1825 by Marc Isambard Brunel to tunnel under the Thames River in London. Modern tunnel boring machines, such as those used to construct the Guadarrama Tunnel, have a tunneling shield at the front, just behind the revolving **cutting head**. It holds the tunnel in shape until concrete lining blocks are locked in place.

SMART TUNNEL

The SMART Tunnel in Kuala Lumpur, Malaysia, is the first tunnel of its kind anywhere in the world. SMART stands for Stormwater Management and Road Tunnel. This tunnel solves two of Kuala Lumpur's problems—traffic jams and flash floods. The city suffers from flooding problems because two major rivers, the Klang and the Gombak, meet in the city center. The SMART tunnel eases the traffic congestion and also carries floodwater away from the city.

It took more than three years for two German-made boring machines to complete digging the SMART Tunnel.

FACT FILE

- Length: 5.9 mi. (9.5 km)
- Where in the world: Kuala Lumpur, Malaysia
- When built: 2007
- Type: Road and storm drain
- Constructed by: Boring

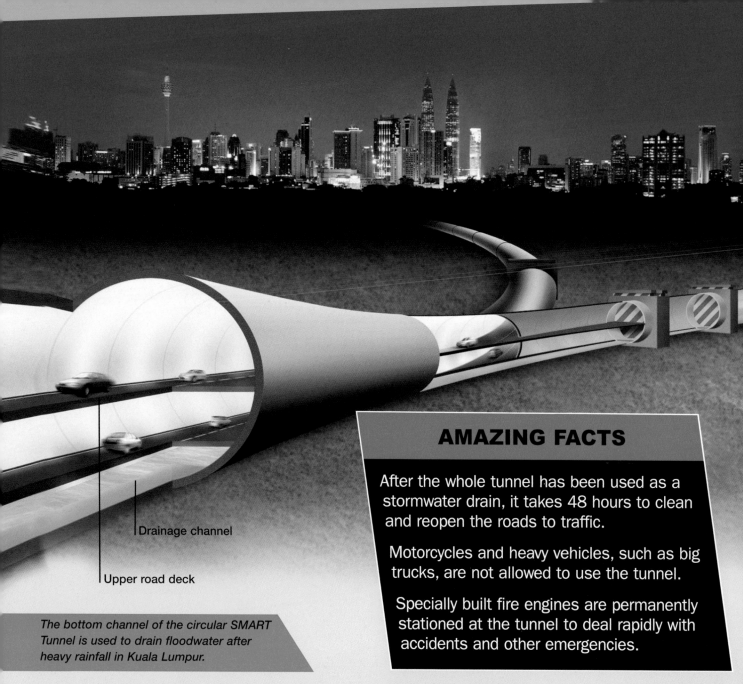

Drainage channel

Upper road deck

The bottom channel of the circular SMART Tunnel is used to drain floodwater after heavy rainfall in Kuala Lumpur.

AMAZING FACTS

After the whole tunnel has been used as a stormwater drain, it takes 48 hours to clean and reopen the roads to traffic.

Motorcycles and heavy vehicles, such as big trucks, are not allowed to use the tunnel.

Specially built fire engines are permanently stationed at the tunnel to deal rapidly with accidents and other emergencies.

Dual-purpose Tunnel

The tunnel was originally designed to be just a stormwater drain. The engineers quickly realized that the same tunnel could carry traffic when it was not needed as a drain. So, a double-deck highway was built inside it! The tunnel was dug by tunnel boring machines. In 2004, two machines started at the middle of the tunnel and set off in opposite directions toward each end. One finished in 2006, the other a little later in 2007.

Road or Drain

The tunnel is used in three ways, or modes. In mode 1, when there is little or no rain, no water is sent down the tunnel and the road decks are open to traffic. In mode 2, water is sent down the bottom of the tunnel and the two road decks above are kept open to traffic. In mode 3, when there is heavy rain, the road decks are closed and doors are opened to let floodwater escape through the tunnel. The tunnel works in mode 3, closed to traffic, once or twice a year.

TUNNELS IN THE FUTURE

Tunnel builders use the lessons learned from past tunnels to build longer and longer tunnels. At almost 33.5 miles (54 km), Japan's Seikan Tunnel is the longest built so far. But even longer tunnels are planned for the future.

A drilling jumbo drills holes for explosives to blast out another section of the new Gotthard Base Tunnel.

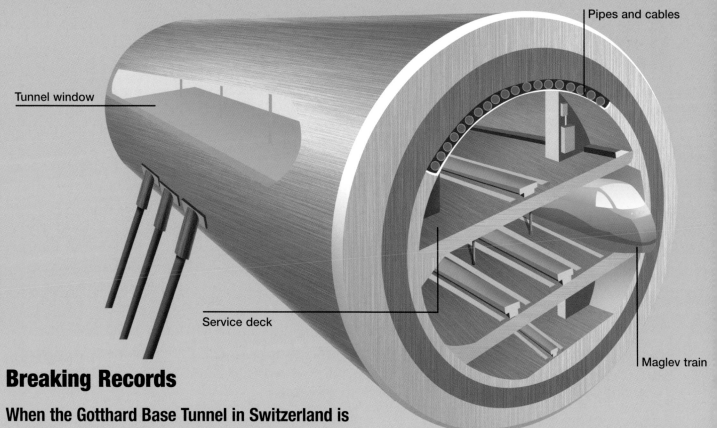

Tunnel window

Pipes and cables

Service deck

Maglev train

A transatlantic tunnel would be anchored securely to the ocean floor by huge cables.

Breaking Records

When the Gotthard Base Tunnel in Switzerland is completed in about 2017, it will be the new record holder at 35 miles (57 km) long. It will form part of a new high-speed rail link between Zürich, Switzerland, and Milan, Italy. Even longer tunnels are being planned. Further in the future, there are plans to build a tunnel between Russia and Alaska under the Bering Strait. When finished, this will approach 64 miles (103 km) in length, which is twice as long as the Channel Tunnel.

Transatlantic Tunnel?

The most amazing tunnel project, even further in the future, is a link between Europe and the United States under the Atlantic Ocean. This project would use high-speed magnetic trains called **maglevs** that float above their track, called a **guideway**. The air would be drawn out of the tunnel to give the trains a top speed of 4,970 miles (8,000 km) per hour. At that speed, a journey between London and New York City, which takes about seven hours by plane today, would take just over an hour!

AMAZING FACTS

A tunnel from Russia to the United States would cost about $65 billion to build.

Up to 99 million tons (90 million t) of freight a year could easily be carried using a Russia-to-America tunnel.

A transatlantic tunnel would be 215 times longer than the Seikan Tunnel and cost more than 3,000 times as much— an astonishing $12 trillion.

GLOSSARY

barge
flat-bottomed boat used for transporting goods or large, heavy cargo, such as parts of tunnels

Big Dig
massive engineering project in Boston, Massachusetts, that moved the main highway through the city into underground tunnels

chalk marl
type of rock containing chalk and clay that is good for tunneling through by means of a tunnel boring machine

concrete
building material made from a mixture of sand, cement, gravel, and water that can be molded into any shape as a liquid and then sets as hard as rock

cut-and-cover
method for building a tunnel near the ground surface by digging a trench the size of the tunnel and then covering it

cutting head
front of a tunnel boring machine with hard picks or teeth that dig into the rock as the cutting head revolves

detonated
exploded

drilling jumbo
machine used by tunnelers to drill holes in rock for explosives

dry dock
a dock that can be kept dry during the construction or repairing of ships

ferries
ships that carry passengers back and forth across a body of water

fixed link
bridge or tunnel, or a combination of the two, that permanently connects two places

freight
goods transported from place to place by road, rail, sea, or air

grout
thin, cement-like liquid used to fill small spaces when it is pumped behind tunnel linings to fill the gap between the rock and lining or into cracked rock to strengthen it

guideway
track or channel along which a maglev train moves

immersed tube
method for building a tunnel in water by lowering a concrete or metal tube onto the seabed or riverbed

lane
part of a road used by a single line of traffic

lay-by
space at the side of the road where drivers can pull over and stop for a while

lining
brick, metal, or concrete material that covers the inside of most tunnels today

lining segment
one part of a tunnel's lining

maglev
type of train that uses powerful magnetic forces to float above its track

pilot tunnel
small tunnel drilled or dug ahead of a main tunnel to check how good or poor the rock is

roadway
road, especially the part of a road's surface, on which traffic is driven

service train
train connected to the back end of a tunnel boring machine for moving spoil back from the machine and building the tunnel lining

service tunnel
small tunnel alongside a main rail or road tunnel for workers to travel through, which also acts as an emergency escape route for travelers

spoil
rock and earth removed to create a tunnel

strait
narrow channel of sea between areas of land

subway
underground passenger railway system

third rail
an extra rail that supplies electric current to a train

tunnel boring machine (TBM)
machine with a revolving cutting head at the front for tunneling through the ground

tunneling shield
structure that supports a newly dug tunnel and protects workers from collapsing rock or earth until a strong lining can be put in place

ventilation
supplying fresh air and getting rid of stale air and fumes

walkway
a passage along the side of a road or rail track where people can walk

water table
the natural level of water in the ground

INDEX

WEB LINKS

http://science.howstuffworks.com/tunnel.htm
Find out more about tunnels and how they are constructed.

http://mta.info/mta/centennial.htm
Read the history of New York City's subway system.

www.discoverychannel.co.uk/machines_and_engineering/tunnels/index.shtml
Read details of the Channel Tunnel between Britain and France.

www.masspike.com/bigdig/background/twt_built.html
See, step-by-step, how the Ted Williams Tunnel under Boston Harbor was built.